FROM THE MISTS OF
LOST KRYPTON, STORIES
ARE TOLD OF TWO MYTHICAL
HEROES WHO TIME AND TIME
AGAIN ROSE TO PROTECT
THEIR PEOPLE FROM
TYRANNY AND
TERROR --

"...I'LL EXPECT IT ON MY DESK TOMORROW..."

"...?"

"...WELL THEN MAKE SOMETHING UP..."

"...YES, COLLEEN, EVEN SUPRMAN. ESPECIALLY SUPRMAN..."

"...A WHOLE SERIES, A FREAKIN' EXPOSE ABOUT THE THREAT THAT KRYPTONIANS AND NEW KRYPTON POSE TO EVERY MAN, WOMAN, AND CHILD ON EARTH..."

DAILY PLANET

"...NO, I THINK SHE KNOWS HOW TO SELL PAPERS, AND I WANT TO HIRE HER... EXACTLY..."

"...LISTEN, THERE WAS ANOTHER PIECE FROM THAT RAG IN METROPOLIS ABOUT SUPERGIRL, SAME WRITER, CAT SOMETHING..."

"...WELL, SUNDAY HERE, SO SATURDAY THERE, YEH? AND NO, I DON'T CARE WHAT TIME IT IS..."

"COLLEEN? IT'S CARTER... YES, YOUR BOSS..."

empire commr
net

empire communications
network

SYDNEY, AUSTRALIA.

THE SLEEPERS PART ONE
EDDY BARROWS <PENCILLER>
RUY JOSÉ   JÚLIO FERREIRA <INKERS>

WHAT CAME BEFORE

It began with an epic battle between Earth's greatest hero, SUPERMAN, and the evil alien BRAINIAC. During that clash, Superman discovered the lost CITY OF KANDOR trapped in the depths of the alien's ship, 100,000 Kryptonian inhabitants inside. Superman was reunited with his people, but at a huge personal cost: he was unable to save the life of his adoptive father, JONATHAN KENT.

Kandor was freed and relocated to Earth, but the uneasy alliance between humans and Kryptonians quickly degenerated into violence and tragedy. A secret government organization, PROJECT 7734, helped orchestrate the aggression between the two races. 7734's leader is GENERAL SAM LANE, a man thought long dead, and he gave the order to assassinate ZOR-EL, SUPERGIRL's father and the leader of the Kryptonians. Meanwhile, a team of Kryptonians brutally murdered several of Metropolis's SCIENCE POLICE on American soil.

In an effort to resolve the growing conflict, Zor-El's widow, ALURA, took charge of the Kryptonians and combined Brainiac's technology with Kandor's to create a new planet — NEW KRYPTON. The planet established an orbit opposite Earth's own. It appeared that the conflict had ended… but looks can be deceiving.

When Alura released GENERAL ZOD from the Phantom Zone and gave him command of New Krypton's army, Superman was forced to make the hardest decision of his life: he would move to New Krypton to keep Zod in check.

Amid the escalating tensions and Superman's absence, new and old heroes alike have risen to protect the Earth.

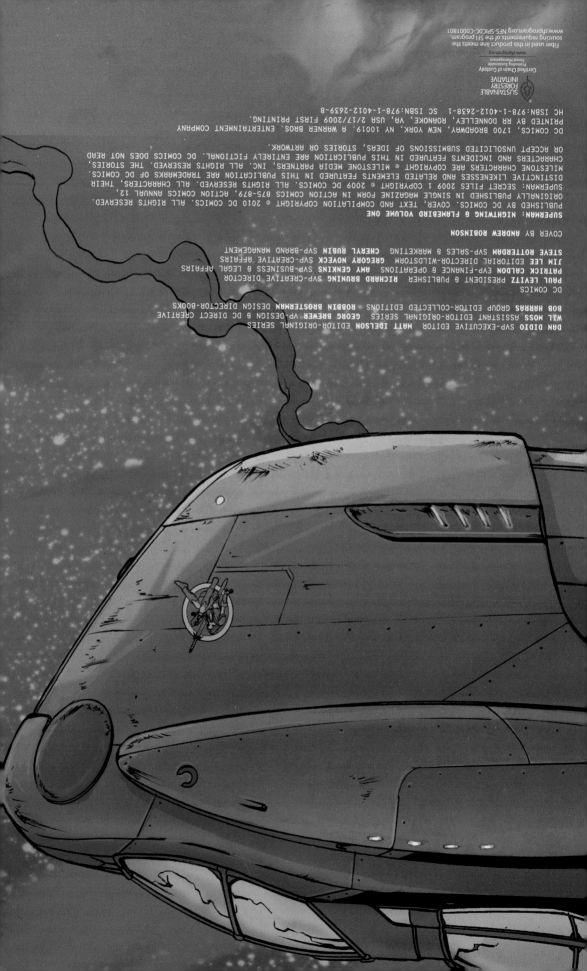

DAN DIDIO SVP-EXECUTIVE EDITOR   MATT IDELSON EDITOR-ORIGINAL SERIES
WIL MOSS ASSISTANT EDITOR-ORIGINAL SERIES   GEORG BREWER VP-DESIGN & DC DIRECT CREATIVE
BOB HARRAS GROUP EDITOR-COLLECTED EDITIONS   ROBBIN BROSTERMAN DESIGN DIRECTOR-BOOKS

DC COMICS

PAUL LEVITZ PRESIDENT & PUBLISHER   RICHARD BRUNING SVP-CREATIVE DIRECTOR
PATRICK CALDON EVP-FINANCE & OPERATIONS   AMY GENKINS SVP-BUSINESS & LEGAL AFFAIRS
JIM LEE EDITORIAL DIRECTOR-WILDSTORM   GREGORY NOVECK SVP-CREATIVE AFFAIRS
STEVE ROTTERDAM SVP-SALES & MARKETING   CHERYL RUBIN SVP-BRAND MANAGEMENT

COVER BY ANDREW ROBINSON

DC COMICS, 1700 BROADWAY, NEW YORK, NY 10019. A WARNER BROS. ENTERTAINMENT COMPANY
PRINTED BY RR DONNELLEY, ROANOKE, VA, USA 2/17/2009 FIRST PRINTING.
HC ISBN:978-1-4012-2638-1   SC ISBN:978-1-4012-2639-8

SUSTAINABLE FORESTRY INITIATIVE
Certified Chain of Custody
Promoting Sustainable Forest Management
www.sfiprogram.org
Fiber used in this product line meets the
sourcing requirements of the SFI program.
www.sfiprogram.org NFS-SPICOC-C0001801

SUPERMAN
NIGHTWING AND FLAMEBIRD

GREG RUCKA
WRITER

EDDY BARROWS
SIDNEY TELES
DIEGO OLMOS
PERE PÉREZ
PENCILLERS

RUY JOSÉ
JÚLIO FERREIRA
SANDRO RIBEIRO
DIEGO OLMOS
BIT
PERE PÉREZ
INKERS

ROD REIS
MAZI
COLORISTS

ROB LEIGH
LETTERER

SUPERMAN CREATED BY
JERRY SIEGEL AND
JOE SHUSTER

THE SLEEPERS PART TWO
EDDY BARROWS SIDNEY TELES <PENCILLERS>
RUY JOSÉ JÚLIO FERREIRA <INKERS>

COVER BY ANDREW ROBINSON

TELL YOUR **PARENTS** I SAID HELLO.

..I DON'T WANT TO BE WEAK...

...SHE'S... SHE'S THE ENEMY...

...KILL HER SHE'LL ≿KAFF≾ NEVER STOP CHASING US...

SUPERMAN WOULDN'T.

S-SUPERMAN ≿KAF≾...

...ISN'T HERE...

ALL THE MORE REASON.

MY SON--

THE SLEEPERS PART THREE
SIDNEY TELES ‹PENCILLER›
SANDRO RIBEIRO ‹INKER›

COVER BY ANDREW ROBINSON

--*TWO* OF THEM, AND ONE OF THEM'S DEFINITELY *NOT* A NATURAL REDHEAD, IF YOU GET MY--

`ACQUIRED_TRACK_ACTIVE_ ALT 218.9 SUBJECT_HOSHI. K..`

`DEEEEEEEEEEEEEE`

--*LIEUTENANT!!!*

`ACQUIRED_FAIL_TRACK_NEGATIVE_ ALT 218.9 SUBJECT_HOSHI. K.`

`TRACK_ACTIVE ALPHA 398 SUBJECT_SUPERGIRL`

`TRAC ROME SUBJ`

WHAT THE HELL JUST HAPPENED?!

`ACQUIRED_FAIL_TRACK_ ALT 218.9 SUBJECT_HOSHI.`

`TRACK ACTIVE ECHO 752 SUBJECT_ICON`

`TRACK SUB ON-EL`

DON'T *KNOW* SIR, WE LOST *SIGNAL* ON DOCTOR LIGHT--

`EEEEEEEEEEEEEEEEEEEEEEEEEEEEEEEEEEEEEEE`

`DEEEEEEEEEEEE`

--*SOME* SORT OF *FAULT* OR--

SHUT THAT *DAMN* ALARM OFF!

CAN WE *REACQUIRE?*

NEGATIVE FUNCTION, SIR.

DAMMIT.

LIEUTENANT HOLLISTER...

...RESUMED SATELLITE SURVEILLANCE AS YOU ORDERED.

FOUR MINUTES AGO, KILO-FOUR PINGED ON A *BOGEY* TAKING OFF FROM THE ROOFTOP O THE RESIDENCE.

HEADING WAS DUE NORTH, ACCELERATIO AND CLIMB RATE *CONSISTENT* WITH THE KRYPTONIAN FLIGHT PROFILE.

IF YOU'RE ABOUT TO TELL ME *SUPERMAN* HAS COME *BACK* TO *EARTH*, LIEUTENANT, I'M GOING TO WANT A *DAMN* GOOD REASON AS TO HOW WE *MISSED* THAT.

NO, SIR. THIS IS SOMETHING *ELSE*.

RIGHT AFTER TAKEOFF, SERGEANT HART RECONN THE KILO-FOUR FOR A *CLOSER* LOOK.

DEET

DEET

DEET

DEET

THE *ARMOR* MATCHES THAT WORN BY ONE OF THE TWO *FLYERS* SPOTTED IN *SYDNEY* BEFORE CARTER'S DISAPPEARANCE.

DEET

WE *MATCHED* HER FACE TO FOOTAGE TAKEN WHEN THE KRYPTONIAN DELEGATION MET WITH THE PRESIDENT.**

WE'VE *ID'ED* HER AS THARA AK-VAR.

HEAD OF SECURITY FOR ALURA ZOR-EL, THE *RULER* OF NEW KRYPTON.

THE SLEEPERS PART FOUR
DIEGO OLMOS <ARTIST>

COVER BY ANDREW ROBINSON

NEW MEXICO.

NORNOK NOK

HELLO? MAY I *HELP* YOU?

WE CERTAINLY *HOPE* SO.

WE LIKE YOUR HOUSE.

DOES IT HAVE A BED?

A *BIG* BED?

WHAT?

WE WANT A HOUSE WITH A *BIG* BED.

I'M *SORRY*, IS THIS SUPPOSED TO BE *FUNNY*?

WELL, NOT TO *YOU*.

TRYING TO GET A LITTLE QUALITY TIME WITH MY GIRL, HERE!

SON OF A--

SHOOT THEM SHOOT--

KRAKKRAKKRAKKRAKKRAKKRAKKRAKKRAKKRAK

--THEM--

NOW, THEN, NADIRA...

...WHERE WERE WE?

...BUT I'M PRETTY *SURE* I *UNDERSTOOD* THAT, NO PROBLEM.

CHRIS HAD TO TAKE CARE OF SOMETHING, HE'LL BE BACK *SOON*.

IT'S ALL RIGHT, THARA. YOU'RE *SAFE* HERE.

NO, NO, I HAVE TO FIND HIM--

WHOA, THERE--

--IT'S NOT *SAFE* IF WE--

--ARE AP-APART...

OKAY, LET'S GET YOU *BACK* IN THE BED, KIDDO...

...YOU'RE *STILL* RECOVERING, YOU NEED TO TAKE IT *SLOW*.

YOU NEARLY *DIED*, THARA.

I...SHE STABBED ME...

...WHO *ARE* YOU?

I'M LOIS.

I'M KIND OF CHRIS'S *MOM*.

YOU...THAT'S *NOT* POSSIBLE.

I HOPE THAT'S BECAUSE YOU THINK I LOOK TOO *YOUNG.*

YOU ARE *HUMAN.*

AND THERE'S *THAT,* YEAH.

I SAID "KIND OF," NOT THAT I *WAS...*

...AND IT *ISN'T* BIOLOGY *ALONE* THAT MAKES SOMEONE A *PARENT.*

BEING RAISED IN KANDOR, I'D THINK YOU'D HAVE *LEARNED* THAT.

HOW DO YOU KNOW I'M FROM KANDOR?

BASIC MATH, KIDDO.

YOU'RE KRYPTONIAN, YOU'RE FROM ONE OF TWO PLACES. AND I DON'T SEE A *PRISON* TATTOO ON YOUR *NECK.*

BESIDES, I WAS THERE WHEN THE KANDOR DELEGATION MET THE PRESIDENT.

YOU LOOK LIKE YOU'RE FEELING BETTER.

YOU SHOULD GET CLEANED UP, PUT THESE ON...

...THEN YOU CAN TELL ME ALL ABOUT WHAT YOU'VE BEEN GETTING *UP* TO WITH MY *SON.*

OLLISTER. WHAT'VE OU GOT FOR ME?"

I'D LIKE TO TRY ONE OF *THOSE*, PLEASE.

YOU WANT THE WORKS?

"YOUR, *uh...FRIEND* SHOULD BE IN METROPOLIS *NOW*, DOING WHATEVER IT IS SHE *DOES*."

"LET ME KNOW WHEN SHE'S BACK. WHAT'S THE *RECON* STATUS?"

"AS PER YOUR ORDERS, GENERAL, RECOVERY TEAMS WERE INSERTED ON SITE FOLLOWING THE UAV STRIKE ON THE KRYPTONIAN MALE DETERMINED TO BE WORKING WITH THARA AK-VAR.

"TEAM ALPHA WAS ABLE TO TAKE A *BLOOD* SAMPLE OFF THE ICE SHEET WHERE THE K WENT *DOWN...*"

"THE WORKS."

WHAT A WONDERFUL TURN OF *PHRASE*.

"...WHILE TEAM BRAVO WAS ABLE TO EFFECT ENTRY TO THE STRUCTURE VIA A PREVIOUSLY SUSTAINED BREACH."

A RAG...

"...AT WHICH TIME THEY DISCOVERED THE *BODY* OF THE MISSING EMPIRE COMMUNICATIONS CEO, DAVID CARTER."

WARNING.

...A BONE...

"BRAVO MANAGED TO RECOVER THE BODY BEFORE LOCAL DEFENSES WENT *ACTIVE*."

YOU ARE *TRESPASSING ON* PRIVATE PROPERTY. *WARNING.*

SECURITY COUNTERMEASURES ARE IN EFFECT.

...A HANK OF HAIR...

"THE TEAM MADE *IMMEDIATE* EXFIL, COMPLETE TO SAFE *RECOVERY*."

"YOU HAVE THE *ANALYSIS?*"

SO AK-VAR AND THIS OTHER K ARE WORKING TOGETHER, TRYING TO *HIDE* WHAT THEY ARE BEHIND THAT *ARMOR*.

THEY'RE *SLEEPERS*, THEY'RE HERE TO *DISRUPT* AND *DECEIVE*.

THEN WHY KILL CARTER?

HE WAS *ANOTHER* SLEEPER, DEEP COVER. EXPLAINS WHY HIS *HISTORY* FALLS APART IF YOU GO BACK MORE THAN A COUPLE OF *YEARS*.

THERE MUST'VE BEEN A *FALLING OUT*. "CARTER" WOUNDED AK-VAR, THAT'S WHY DOCTOR LIGHT HAD TO *TREAT* HER.

FIGURE OUR UNNAMED K MURDERED HIM IN RESPONSE.

IF THAT'S *TRUE*, IT MEANS YOUR *DAUGHTER* ISN'T JUST *SYMPATHETIC* TO THE Ks.

IT MEANS SHE'S *INVOLVED*, SHE'S PART OF THEIR *OPERATION*.

IT MEANS SHE'S A *TRAITOR*, LIEUTENANT. SHE'S *AIDING* KRYPTONIAN *SPIES* ON EARTH.

THERE *IS* ANOTHER POSSIBILITY, SIR. IF CARTER WAS A SLEEPER, PERHAPS AK-VAR AND HER *PARTNER* WERE TRYING TO *STOP* HIM.

THEY MAY BE TRYING TO *HELP* US.

THEY CAN MAKE *DIAMONDS* OUT OF *COAL* WITH THEIR BARE *HANDS*, LIEUTENANT...

...DO YOU *REALLY* THINK THEY'VE EVEN THE *SLIGHTEST* INCLINATION TO BE OUR *FRIENDS*?

DEET DEET

GENERAL LANE.

SIR? WATCH OFFICER...

...WE'VE *FOUND* THEM...

WHERE?

NEW MEXICO, SIR. WE'RE STILL TRYING TO SORT IT OUT.

LAW ENFORCEMENT RESPONDED TO SOMETHING OUT AT A LOCAL CONGRESSMAN'S PLACE, FOUND THE HOUSE *TOTALED...*

...BODY COUNT IS *FOUR* SHERIFF'S DEPUTIES *DEAD* PLUS THE CONGRESSMAN'S *WIFE*, ENCASED IN ICE.

WE *HACKED* THE *VIDEO CAMERA* ON ONE OF THE SHERIFF'S CARS, IF YOU'LL LOOK AT MONITOR SEVEN...

...YOU CAN SEE THESE TWO *FLYING* AWAY.

STILL THINK THEY'RE TRYING TO *HELP* US, LIEUTENANT?

WE'VE HAD *NO* REPORTS OF AK-VAR LEAVING YOUR DAUGHTER'S RESIDENCE IN METROPOLIS--

THAT DOESN'T MEAN SHE'S STILL *THERE*. ALL THAT MEANS IS SHE *MADE* THE SURVEILLANCE.

GET A COPY OF THE FOOTAGE TO THE *MOUTHPIECE* FOR PROPAGANDA USE, AND PUT THE RECOVERY TEAM ON STANDBY.

SOON AS WE HAVE A PROJECTION ON THEIR HEADING, SEND THE TEAM *OUT*. THEY HAVE *FULL FORCE* AUTHORIZATION...

...I WANT THOSE *SPIES* CAUGHT, INTERROGATED, AND *BROKEN...*

"...AND I DON'T CARE HOW."

...RESCUED HIM FROM THE PHANTOM ZONE?

URSA AND ZOD HAD HIM PRISONER. I...I FREED HIM.

IF YOU WERE IN KANDOR, HOW'D YOU KNOW HE WAS THERE?

HE TOLD ME. IN MY DREAMS.

YOUR DREAMS?

YES.

HE SPOKE TO YOU IN YOUR DREAMS?

I KNOW HOW IT SOUNDS.

IT'S THE TRUTH.

I DON'T DOUBT--

--IT--

K'RISS! I WAS WORRIED ABOUT YOU.

I WAS WORRIED ABOUT YOU.

Ahem...

...WHAT KEPT YOU?

I'M SORRY, MOM, I GOT BACK AS SOON AS I COULD. I GOT ATTACKED, AND THEN I HAD TO--

ATTACKED? AT THE FORTRESS--

URSA WAS *STILL* THERE? SHE WAS--

NO, I MEAN *YES*, BUT...

...URSA *WAS* THERE, SHE'D *MURDERED* TOR-AN. SHE WAS *AFRAID* HE'D *TALK*.

THEN WE *HEARD* THESE... *MACHINES* IN THE *AIR*. SHE *RAN*, AND THEY *ATTACKED* ME, AND THEN I HAD TO GO BACK AND GET *THESE*.

MACHINES? WHAT *KIND* OF MACHINES?

LIKE LITTLE JET PLANES. TWO OF THEM.

SOMEONE SENT UAVs AFTER YOU?

UAVs? WHAT'S THAT?

UNMANNED AERIAL VEHICLES...

...BUT THAT'S *MILITARY* TECHNOLOGY...

LOOK!

...'T'S
I-?#0 !0⎕!
◇!⎕!-◇!!/

WHAT?
WHERE?

HOLD ON--

IT'S AZ-REL AND NADIRA!

--OF THE
CONGRESSMAN'S
NEW MEXICO HOME
WITH *FREEZE* BREATH
AND *TOTAL*
DESTRUCTION?!?

THIS COUPLE IS
LOOSE ON EARTH, RIGHT
NOW! AND IF THEY *ARE*
KRYPTONIANS, THEN THE
ONLY QUESTION IS...

...*WHERE* WILL THEY
STRIKE NEXT? THIS IS
MORGAN EDGE...

WHO--

WE'LL BE
BACK.

I'LL BE
HERE.

...HELLO, COMMANDER HARPER?
THIS IS LOIS LANE, FROM THE
DAILY PLANET...

...OH, I HAVE
EVERYONE'S
NUMBER. LISTE
I'M WONDERING
YOU COULD HE
ME WITH A
FAVOR...

OH! OH, I SEE A BIG ONE!

YOU WANT IT? HOLD ON...

YOU DIDN'T!
LET ME SEE!

OF COURSE I DID. ANYTHING FOR YOU...

THERE'S A SAYING ON THIS PLANET...

...ALL YOU HAVE TO DO IS ASK FOR IT, BABY.

...GET A ROOM.

THEY'RE WEARING THE SYMBOLS OF NIGHTWING AND FLAMEBIRD, JUST LOOK AT THAT.

SOMEBODY'S BEEN READING TOO MANY FAIRY TALES.

OOOH, THAT MEANS THERE'S ONE FOR EACH OF US--

DON'T YOU HURT HER!!!

NNHAAAAA!!!!

NO--

WHUMMMP

--I'LL LEAVE THAT TO YOU!

WHEN I SAID "GET A ROOM"--

INTERESTING. THERE WAS ONLY SUPPOSED TO BE *TWO* OF YOU...

--I MEANT WE HAD ONE WAITING FOR YOU.

THE SLEEPERS PART FIVE
DIEGO OLMOS ‹PENCILLER›
DIEGO OLMOS   BIT ‹INKERS›

COVER BY ANDREW ROBINSON

THIS *IS* PRETTY.

FOUR FOR THE *PRICE* OF TWO.

GO GET THEM.

ALL OF THEM.

WAIT! WHOEVER YOU ARE, *LISTEN* TO ME!

WE'RE *NOT* YOUR ENEMY--

--WE'RE TRYING TO *HELP* YOU!

THOSE TWO--

--THEY'RE YOUR *ENEMY* NOT US!

!!--⟨⟩◇! ⟨⟩⟨⟩⟨⟩-!

AZ-REL! HELP!

YOU'RE KRYPTONIANS.

YOU'RE ALL THE ENEMY.

NIGHTWING--

THERE'RE TOO MANY OF THEM!

THIS ISN'T OUR FIGHT--

--IT'S THEIRS!

THEN LET'S GET OUT OF HERE!

GET OFF ME--

--NIGHTWING--

--THEY'RE GETTING AWAY!

HOLD ON, I'LL--

NO! DON'T WORRY ABOUT ME!

DON'T LET THEM ESCAPE!

GO--

--I'LL CATCH UP!

RAO, SHIELD ME!

GRAB HER HEAD!

GET THAT HELMET OFF HER!

LET ME GO!

IT'S THE OTHER TWO, THE ONES YOU JUST LET ESCAPE, THEY'RE THE ONES YOU SHOULD BE FIGHTING!

SHUT HER UP.

YOUR BOYFRIEND... WHAT'S HIS NAME?...

...FEEL THAT EMOTION, YOU'RE BURNING WITH IT...

...NADIRA AND... AND AZ-REL... AND YOUR BOYFRIEND...

...CHRIS, THERE IT IS... OH, OH THAT'S SWEET...

LET'S *SEE* WHAT'S ON YOUR *MIND*, SHALL WE, GIRL?

...WHO ARE THE *OTHER* TWO?...

...*HOW* MANY MORE OF YOU ARE THERE?... ...THAT'S *RIGHT*, THAT'S IT...

...BUT IT'LL *NEVER* HAPPEN, THARA, YOU'LL *NEVER* BE IN HIS *ARMS*...

...TELL YOU *WHAT*, I'LL MAKE YOU A *DEAL*...

...WHEN WE *KILL* HIM, I'LL MAKE SURE YOU'RE *WATCHING*--

YOU WILL NOT HARM HIM!
NEVER AGAIN WILL WE LET YOU HARM HIM!

WE ARE NOT VENGEFUL.

BUT WE WILL FIGHT TO DEFEND WHAT IS OURS, WHAT WE LOVE.

YOU ARE WARNED.

CRYPTIC TWO-TWO, THIS IS *RETRIEVAL.*

GOT A *MESSAGE* FOR THE GENERAL...

...WE MAY HAVE A WHOLE *NEW* PROBLEM...

YOU SAY THAT, YET YOUR LOVE FOR THE FLAMEBIRD IS LEGENDARY!

WILL YOU DIE FOR HER THIS TIME? OR IS IT HER TURN TO DIE FOR YOU?

I DON'T KNOW WHAT YOU TWO ARE TALKING ABOUT--

IT DOESN'T MATTER--

--THIS TIME YOU DIE ALONE!

NO--

--THE PEOPLE--

--HNNN

◊◊♦⬧'⬧ ◊♦⬧ ⬧--

♦♦⬧ ⬧-◊◊! ◊♦⬧'⬧ ⬧▮▮ ▯▮▮-▮◊⬧ ⬧♦⬧ ▮▮-⬧◊♦⬧ ⬧♦⬧ ◊♦◊◊!

LET'S FINISH HIM--

NEXT TIME! LET'S GO BEFORE THE OTHERS GET HERE!

NIGHTWING! *WHERE* ARE *YOU?*

HERE! I CAN'T *HOLD* IT-

--QUIC GET TH PEOPL CLEAR

GOT THEM!

NIGHTWING? I'VE *GOT*--

KABOOM

NIGHTWING! *NIGHTWING!*

◇▥, ◇▥, ◇-□☼!◇☼--

IT'S *ALL* RIGHT...

RAO, NO, PLEASE--

...I'M ALL RIGHT...

...NADIRA AND AZ-REL *FLED* TOWARDS THE *CITY.* WE SHOULD FOLLOW THEM.

...YEAH.

SAMUEL L
LANE
IOWA
GENERAL OF
THE ARMY
IMPERIEX W
NOV 1
SEPT

MISS LANE?

HELLO, MON-EL.

COMMANDER HARPER GAVE YOU MY *MESSAGE*?

YES, HE DID. HE SAID YOU NEED MY *ASSISTANCE*?

I NEED YOU TO *LOOK* AT SOMETHING FOR ME.

OR, MORE PRECISELY, LOOK *INTO* SOMETHING.

THE *STONE*?

WHAT THAT STONE MARKS, WHAT *ALL* THESE PIECES OF *MARBLE* MARK, IS *GRAVES*, MON-EL.

THIS IS ARLINGTON NATIONAL CEMETERY. IT'S WHERE THE UNITED STATES BURIES AND REMEMBERS ITS SOLDIERS.

THERE ARE SO MANY.

THIS IS MY **FATHER'S** GRAVE.

YOU HAVE MY **CONDOLENCES.**

I MAY NOT **NEED** THEM.

TELL ME WHAT YOU **SEE.**

THERE IS A BOX OF SOME SORT, SEVERAL FEET DOWN... BONES IN IT, THOSE OF AN ADULT HUMAN MALE.

LOOK AT THE LEFT WRIST, THERE SHOULD BE--

A SMALL PIECE OF **METAL.** A **SCREW,** I BELIEVE, HOLDING ONE OF THE BONES TO **ANOTHER.**

YEAH, YOU'D **BE** THAT THOROUGH, WOULDN'T YOU, DAD?

CAN YOU SEE THE **TEETH?**

YES. COUNT THEM.

...THIRTY-TWO.

HOW MANY?

THIRTY-TWO TEETH. IS THAT **WRONG?**

DAD HAD ALL FOUR **WISDOM** TEETH OUT WHEN I WAS **SIX.** LAID HIM UP FOR TWO **DAYS.** MY FATHER HAD TWENTY-EIGHT TEETH.

THAT'S **NOT** THE BODY OF GENERAL SAM LANE.

MY FATHER IS **ALIVE.**

WHAT DO YOU **MEAN**, YOU **LOST** THEM?

YOU JUST SAID ONE OF THEM WAS **ON FIRE**!

THEIR **TRAJECTORY** OUT OF DEATH VALLEY TOOK THEM **STRAIGHT** INTO **LOS ANGELES**, SIR!

YOU ORDERED US TO KEEP A LOW PROFILE, NOT TO REVEAL OURSELVES TO THE CIVILIAN AUTHORITIES! WE **HAD** TO ABANDON **PURSUIT**!

I SENT YOU OUT TO GET **TWO** OF THEM, YOU FOUND **FOUR**, YOU BAGGED **NONE**!

MAYBE **MORE** THAN **FOUR**, SIR...

...I WAS IN AK-VAR'S HEAD WHEN SHE... **IMMOLATED**...

...AND I WASN'T IN THERE **ALONE**.

WHAT DOES THAT EVEN **MEAN**?

I CAN ONLY PICK UP **SURFACE** THOUGHTS. WHEN THIS **OTHER** THING MANIFESTED, IT WAS LIKE IT HAD BEEN THERE THE **WHOLE** TIME...

...I'VE **NEVER** ENCOUNTERED ANYTHING LIKE IT BEFORE.

RETURN TO **BASE** IMMEDIATELY.

MAYBE YOU CAN MANAGE **THAT** WITHOUT SCREWING IT **UP**.

DO WE SEND A **GROUND** TEAM?

AND **RISK** A FULL-BLOWN **BATTLE** IN THE MIDDLE OF THE **MEDIA CAPITAL** OF THE **WORLD**?

YOU KNOW THE **PLAN**, WE'RE **NOT** READY TO GO **OVERT** JUST YET--

--WHERE THE HELL DID HER *ROYAL HIGHNESS* GO?

SIR?

MIRABAI! SHE WAS *JUST* HERE!

ALERT *SECURITY,* I WANT A *FULL SWEEP,* SHE *KNOWS* SHE'S NOT SUPPOSED TO BE--

I'M BACK.

HOLLISTER

WHERE THE *HELL* DID YOU *GO?*

TO DO WHAT YOU *WOULDN'T,* GENERAL.

YOU *ALLOW* YOUR ENEMY TO *HIDE* BEHIND CIVILIANS. I *KNOW* THE *PRICE* OF THAT.

I'M ALLOWING *NOTHING.* I'M *BIDING* MY *TIME.*

AND HOW MANY *MORE* OF YOUR PEOPLE WOULD *PERISH* BECAUSE YOU CHOOSE TO *BIDE* YOUR *TIME?*

I KNOW *THAT* PRICE, TOO.

IF YOU'VE *JEOPARDIZED* THE OPERATION--

OF COURSE NOT.

BUT THOSE *OTHER* TWO AREN'T *PART* OF THE OPERATION, ARE THEY?

WHAT THE *HELL* DID YOU *DO?*

SEE FOR YOURSELF.

NADIRA...

YOU'RE WELCOME, GENERAL.

THE END?

THE ORIGIN OF NIGHTWING AND FLAMEBIRD
PERE PÉREZ <ARTIST>

COVER BY RENATO GUEDES

THIS IS A STORY ABOUT DESTINY.

THE CALL TO MOBILIZE COMES IN THE PREDAWN HOURS.

IT TAKES THE UNIT CALLED BLACK ZERO LESS THAN FOUR MINUTES TO DEPLOY.

IT'S HARD TO HEAR. THE TRANSPORT IS RUNNING FLAT OUT, THE ENGINES SCREAMING, THE HULL RATTLING. EACH SOLDIER STRAINS TO HEAR THEIR COMMANDER'S WORDS.

WHAT THEY HEAR ISN'T GOOD.

SOME FIFTY MINUTES AGO, A SURPRISE ATTACK WAS LAUNCHED AGAINST ONE OF THE LARGEST CITIES ON THE PLANET, ALIEN IN ORIGIN. NO ONE KNOWS WHO. NO ONE KNOWS WHY.

CIVIL DEFENSE COLLAPSED WITHIN MINUTES. CASUALTIES ARE ESTIMATED AT THE TENS OF THOUSANDS.

PEOPLE--THEIR PEOPLE, THE PEOPLE THEY'VE SWORN TO PROTECT AND TO SERVE--ARE DYING.

THEY LISTEN TO EVERY WORD THEIR COMMANDER SAYS.

THEY TRUST HER. THEY BELIEVE IN HER.

IF ANYONE IS GOING TO GET THEM OUT OF THIS ALIVE, IT'S HER.

SHE TELLS THEM WHERE THEY'RE GOING.

OUR TARGET IS KANDOR.

KANDOR IS THEIR CAPITAL, THE SEAT OF THE PLANETARY GOVERNMENT. THE THIRD-LARGEST CITY ON THE PLANET, WITH A POPULATION OF OVER SEVEN MILLION.

BUT FOR FIRST ASPIRANT TES AK-VAR, SITTING OPPOSITE HER HUSBAND, FEELING EVERY ONE OF THE FIFTY POUNDS OF COMBAT GEAR SHE CARRIES, KANDOR MEANS MORE THAN THAT.

WHEN SHE OFFERS REASSURANCE, IT'S EASY TO BELIEVE HER.

SHE'S THEIR LEADER.

SQUAD, ON YOUR FEET!

IF ANYONE IS GOING TO GET THEM OUT OF THIS ALIVE...

WE ARE THE **BEST** KRYPTON HAS TO **OFFER!**

WE ARE KRYPTON'S **SWORD** AND ITS **SHIELD!**

GENERAL ZOD SENDS **US**, BECAUSE WE WILL GET THE JOB **DONE!**

NOT FOR HIM, **NOT** FOR THE COUNCIL, BUT FOR **OUR PEOPLE!**

...IT'S HER.

BLACK ZERO! TO VICTORY!

THEY HIT THE GROUND RUNNING, WORKING BLOCK TO BLOCK, STREET BY STREET, DEEPER INTO THE HEART OF THE CITY.

THE ENTIRE TIME, THEIR SENSES ARE ASSAULTED BY THE CARNAGE AROUND THEM.

THE AIR REEKS WITH THE SMELL OF BLOOD, SMOKE, AND DEATH.

SCREAMS DISAPPEAR BEHIND EXPLOSIONS, SOBS ECHO AMID THE RUBBLE. PARENTS CALL OUT TO CHILDREN. INFANTS HOWL IN TERROR.

AND EVERYWHERE THEY GO, THEY SEE CORPSES, AND THIS CONFIRMS THEIR WORST FEARS.

THESE ALIENS, THEY'RE HERDING A SEGMENT OF THE POPULACE TO THE CENTER OF THE CITY.

FOR WHAT REASON, NO ONE CAN GUESS.

THOSE THAT AREN'T BEING HERDED ARE BEING CULLED.

TES!

IT IS AN AWFUL, TERRIBLE MOMENT OF RELIEF FOR TES AK-VAR AND HER HUSBAND.

THEIR DAUGHTER IS STILL ALIVE.

BUT THEIR DAUGHTER IS A PRISONER.

TES, AK, YOU'RE WITH ME.

THE REST OF YOU, FLANK AND GIVE COVER.

FOR THARA AK-VAR, IT IS THE PENULTIMATE MOMENT OF A CHILD'S NIGHTMARE.

THWP

KIK KOK KIK KO

HER PARENTS HAVE COME TO SAVE HER.

KIK KOK KIK KOK KIK

SPLTCH

NOW!

MOM! DAD!

KIK KOK KIK

THWP

THWP

THWP

K KOK

IT IS A MOMENT SHE WILL NEVER FORGET.

SVNCH

GVCHH

BLKK

IT TAKES THREE SECONDS, MAYBE FOUR.

KIK KOK KIK KOK KIK

RAO...

AND THEN BLACK ZERO, THE PRIDE OF THE KRYPTONIAN ARMY, IS NO MORE.

KIK KOK KIK

PLEASE

...RAO PLEASE...

MOMMA!

THARA...

COMMANDER--

--HELP US--

--IN THE NAME OF CYTHONNA, *PLEASE*, URSA--

NO *LET GO* OF ME *THARA* MY BABY LET *GO*--

--GKKK

IN THE TERRIFYING DAYS THAT FOLLOW THEIR ABDUCTION, KANDOR STRUGGLES TO RECOVER FROM WHAT HAS HAPPENED.

THE BODIES OF THE DEAD ARE BURNED, THE SOULS OF THE DEPARTED ESCORTED BACK TO RAO ON PRAYERS OF THE RELIGIOUS GUILD.

SLOWLY, THE REALIZATION DAWNS THAT THEIR JAILOR'S INTEREST IN THEM IS LIMITED.

TO BRAINIAC, THE ONE HUNDRED THOUSAND KRYPTONIANS TRAPPED IN THE BOTTLE CITY ARE ANTS IN A FARM, TO BE OBSERVED, NOTHING MORE.

A SMALL COMFORT WHEN FAMILIES HAVE BEEN TORN APART AND SLAUGHTERED, WHEN FRIENDS AND LOVERS HAVE BEEN LOST.

NOT ONE SURVIVOR FAILS TO EXHIBIT SYMPTOMS OF POST-TRAUMATIC STRESS. SLEEP IS PLAGUED WITH NIGHTMARES, DAYS AWASH IN DEPRESSION, IRRATIONAL ANGER, AND SORROW.

FACED WITH AN UNCERTAIN FUTURE, KANDOR STRUGGLES TO RE-ESTABLISH SOME OF WHAT HAS BEEN LOST, TO REBUILD SOME REPLICA OF KRYPTONIAN SOCIETY.

KANDOR'S ORPHANS ARE QUICKLY PLACED INTO DIFFERENT GUILDS.

LIKE HER PARENTS, AND THEIR PARENTS BEFORE THEM, THARA AK-VA... ENTERS SERVICE IN THE MILITARY GUILD.

THE HOPE IS THAT, ONE DAY, SHE AND THE REST OF HER GUILD WILL SEE COMBAT.

THE HOPE IS THAT, ONE DAY, THE PRISONERS OF KANDOR WILL SOMEHOW RISE UP, AND TAKE BACK THEIR FREEDOM.

AND ON THAT DAY, HAVING SECURED VICTORY...

...THEY WILL BE ABLE TO RETURN HOME.

OR YEARS, THIS IS THE HOPE THAT SUSTAINS KANDOR.

UNTIL THE DAY THAT BRAINIAC ENCOUNTERS ANOTHER GROUP OF REFUGEES FROM KRYPTON. ARGO CITY, DRIFTING IN THE VOID.

THE NEW ADDITIONS ARE INCORPORATED INTO THE BOTTLE CITY.

THE NEW ADDITIONS BRING NEWS, AND THE HOPE THAT HAS SUSTAINED KANDOR FINALLY, MISERABLY, DIES IN ITS TELLING.

KRYPTON IS GONE.

THEIR PRISON IS NOW, AND FOREVER WILL BE, THEIR HOME.

FOR THARA AK-VAR, THE NEWS IS HEARTBREAKING, BUT THE MESSENGERS ARE WELCOME.

IN KANDOR, FOR ALL THESE YEARS, SHE HAS BEEN ALONE, BUT NOW SHE SEES PEOPLE SHE KNOWS, THE PARENTS OF HER BEST FRIEND KARA.

THARA AK-VAR HAS LOST HER MOTHER AND FATHER.

ALURA ZOR-EL AND HER HUSBAND HAVE LOST THEIR DAUGHTER.

AND IF EACH OF THEM KNOWS THE FAMILY THEY NOW MAKE IS NOT THE ONE THEY WOULD HAVE CHOSEN...

PERHAPS IT DID.

TO PUNISH HIM, HIS MOTHER WOULD SOMETIMES LOCK HIM OUTSIDE, OFTEN FOR DAYS ON END.

IT CERTAINLY FORCED HIM TO DISCOVER WAYS TO SNEAK INTO AND OUT OF THE PRISON.

BEING SMALL HELPED; HE COULD FIT WHERE THE OTHERS COULD NOT.

MOST OF HIS FIRST SIX YEARS WERE SPENT WITHIN THE PRISON'S WALLS, WHERE CHRIS WAS CONCEIVED AND BORN.

HIDE IN THE PLAC[ES] THEY WOULD NEV[ER] LOOK.

MOST, BUT NOT ALL.

THIS WAS SUPPOSED TO TEACH HIM "SELF-RELIANCE" AND "DISCIPLINE" AND "COURAGE."

IN HIS MIND, HE IS STILL [A] SIX-YEAR-OL[D] BOY.

IN HIS MIND, HE STILL HAS A SIX-YEAR-OLD'S BODY.

WHEN THAT BODY GETS STUCK, CONFUSION QUICKLY TURNS TO FEAR.

TRAPPED, HE STRUGGLES TO FREE HIMSELF, HIS RISING PANIC DESTROYING ANY DESIRE TO REMAIN HIDDEN.

HE SCREAMS FOR HELP, NOT CARING THAT ANY WHO MIGHT HEAR IS AS LIKELY TO TORMENT HIM AS TO AID HIM.

NO HELP COMES.

NOT FOR A LONG TIME.

GENERAL ZOD LED TWENTY-NINE OF FORT ROZ'S PRISONERS IN HIS CONQUEST OF EARTH.

SEVEN DIED IN THE BATTLE TO DRIVE THEM BACK INTO THE PHANTOM ZONE.

OF THE TWENTY-TWO WHO REMAINED, ONLY ONE OF THEM EVER SHOWED CHRISTOPHER ANYTHING APPROACHING KINDNESS.

NON HAS BEEN CALLED MANY THINGS: SIMPLE; A BRUTE; AN ANIMAL; A SAVAGE.

HE WASN'T ALWAYS THAT WAY.

ONCE, HIS MIND WAS AS BRILLIANT AS ANY KRYPTON HAD EVER KNOWN.

ONCE, THAT BRILLIANCE WAS ONLY MATCHED BY HIS COMPASSION.

UNTIL THOSE THINGS WERE STOLEN FROM HIM FOR THE CRIME OF TELLING TRUTH TO POWER.

NON HAS THE DISTINCTION OF BEING THE ONLY PERSON IN FORT ROZ TO TREAT CHRISTOPHER WITH CONSISTENT KINDNESS.

AND IF THEY WERE KINDRED SPIRITS BEFORE, THE CHILD AND THE CHILDLIKE MAN...

...NOW, EVEN MORE SO, THEY SHARE THE SAME PRISONS.

THE PHANTOM ZONE, AND THEIR OWN BODIES.

IN ANOTHER PRISON, ANOTHER PRISONER WRESTLES DEMONS LESS DEFINED.

DAYS HAVE BECOME WEEKS HAVE BECOME YEARS IN KANDOR.

YET EVEN AFTER SO MUCH TIME, SLEEP REMAINS THARA AK-VAR'S ENEMY.

AS A CHILD, FIRE OFTEN PLAYED A PART IN HER DREAMS, AND THIS NEVER ALARMED HER.

FIRE--RAO--IS A CONSTANT IN KRYPTONIAN RELIGION, AND BEFORE THE ABDUCTION, THARA WAS CONSIDERED QUITE DEVOUT.

SOMETHING HER BEST FRIEND, KARA ZOR-EL, OFTEN TEASED HER ABOUT, IN FACT.

BUT WITH THE DEATH OF HER PARENTS, THESE DREAMS HAVE BECOME NIGHTMARES, AND THEY HAVE NEVER GONE AWAY.

IN FACT, THEY HAVE GOTTEN WORSE.

IN THE BEGINNING, THERE WERE ONLY FLAMES.

NOW, THOUGH, THARA PERCEIVES SOMETHING ELSE.

SOMETHING ALIVE WITHIN THE FIRES.

SOMETHING AWESOME AND TERRIBLE AND ANCIENT.

AND IT'S WATCHING HER.

WHEN ZOR-EL, [ELE]CTED WITH ALURA [TO] HEAD KANDOR'S [GO]VERNMENT, ASKED [T]HARA TO BECOME HIS HEAD OF [S]ECURITY, MANY [W]ERE SURPRISED.

CERTAINLY, THERE WERE OTHERS IN THE MILITARY GUILD MORE QUALIFIED.

BUT IN THARA, BOTH ZOR-EL AND ALURA SEE THE MEMORY OF THEIR LOST DAUGHTER.

AND AFTER ALL THAT KANDOR HAS SUFFERED, CAN THEY BE BLAMED FOR CHOOSING SENTIMENT OVER EXPERIENCE?

WHETHER ZOR-EL SAW RELIGIOUS SIGNIFICANCE IN WHAT THARA TOLD HIM WILL NEVER BE KNOWN.

PERHAPS, UNABLE TO OFFER AN ANSWER TO HIS SURROGATE DAUGHTER THROUGH SCIENCE, HE OFFERED PHILOSOPHY.

PERHAPS HE SOUGHT ONLY TO REDIRECT HER TO THE CHURCH SHE HAD SINCE ABANDONED.

WHAT SHE FOUND WAS SOMETHING ELSE ENTIRELY.

PERHAPS HE HOPED THAT, IN RELIGION, THARA MIGHT ONCE AGAIN FIND SOLACE, IF NOT A SOLUTION.

WHAT SHE FOUND WAS A LEGACY.

KRYPTONIAN RELIGIOUS BELIEF HAS BEEN CHARACTERIZED AS POLYTHEISTIC, AKIN TO HINDUISM ON EARTH. THIS IS INACCURATE.

A BETTER ANALOGUE MIGHT BE CATHOLICISM, WITH RAO, THE SUN GOD, AS A MONOTHEISTIC DEITY, SURROUNDED BY NAMED "ANGELS," CYTHONNA, YUDA, AND THE LIKE.

OTHER ASPECTS OF THE RELIGION MIGHT BEST BE LIKENED TO TERRAN CABALS, OR EVEN CULTS, WITH LAYERS OF SECRETS CONCEALING FURTHER MYSTERIES.

THIS MAY EXPLAIN WHY THE RELIGIOUS GUILD IS SO SMALL IN COMPARISON TO THE OTHER GUILDS, AND WHY SO LITTLE IS KNOWN ABOUT THEM.

OUTSIDE THE STANDARD LIFE-CYCLE EVENTS--BIRTH, MARRIAGE, DEATH--MOST KRYPTONIANS HAVE NO INTERACTION WITH THE CLERGY.

AND THE CLERGY ITSELF RARELY INTERACTS WITH THE REST OF SOCIETY.

AK-VAR.

IT SHOULD BE NOTED, HERE, THAT KRYPTONIAN NAMING CONVENTION USES A PERSONAL--"AK"--TO PRECEDE A FAMILIAL--"VAR."

AK-VAR.

AK-VAR.

FOR MALES, THIS SUFFICES. THUS THE HOUSE OF VAR WOUL[D] HAVE SONS NAMED "KEM-VAR" OR "BYN-VAR."

FEMALE NAMES, HOWEVER, TAKE A PERSONAL--"TES" OR "THARA"--TO PRECEDE A HUSBAND OR FATHER--"AK-VAR."

AK-VAR.

AK-VAR.

AK-VAR.

THIS VARIATION MAKES THE GENERATIONAL REPEAT OF A SPECIFIC NAME, IN THIS CASE "AK-VAR," INCREDIBLY RARE.

YES.

TO HEAR THARA AK-VAR TELL IT, THEY KNEW SHE WAS COMING.

TO HEAR THARA AK-VAR TELL IT, THEY HAD BEEN WAITING FOR HER.

SHE BELIEVES--ABSOLUTELY, COMPLETELY, AND SINCERELY BELIEVES--THAT WHAT SHE EXPERIENCED NEXT WAS REAL.

THAT IT WAS NOT A HALLUCINATION. THAT IT WAS NOT SOME MANIPULATION OF SUNSTONES KNOWN ONLY TO THE RELIGIOUS GUILD.

THAT SHE WAS GRANTED A VISION, PERHAPS BY RAO HIMSELF.

THAT THE TRUE FLAMEBIRD APPEARED TO HER IN THE CATHEDRAL, THE HALF-PHOENIX, HALF-DRAGON SENTINEL OF KRYPTONIAN LEGEND.

THAT THE FLAMEBIRD SPOKE TO HER IN THE ANCIENT WAY, MIND TOUCHING MIND...

...AND SHARED ALL HER SORROWS.

THE RELIGIOUS GUILD CLAIMED THARA AK-VAR AS ONE OF THEIR OWN, THEIR RIGHT BY LAW. THEY OFFERED NO EXPLANATION.

FOR HER PART, THARA WENT WILLINGLY, IF NOT WITHOUT FEAR.

--THEN MASKED.

SHE REMEMBERS WEEPING, BOTH FOR HERSELF AND FOR THE FLAMEBIRD, NO LONGER CERTAIN IF THEY WERE NOT, IN FACT, ONE AND THE SAME.

WEEPING FOR WHAT HAD BEEN TAKEN FROM THEM, THEIR FRIEND AND MATE AND LOVER, THE NIGHTWING.

LOST IN SOME UNKNOWN DARKNESS, JUST AS THEY HAD BEEN.

CHRISTOPHER'S ISOLATION IS OF A DIFFERENT SORT ENTIRELY.

WHETHER NON ACTIVELY HID CHRISTOPHER FROM URSA AND ZOD, AS WELL AS THE OTHER PRISONERS, IS UNKNOWN.

WHAT CAN BE INTERPRETED AS DECEPTION CAN JUST AS EASILY BE READ AS A SIN OF OMISSION COMMITTED BY A DAMAGED MIND.

NON'S IMPAIRED FACULTIES, AS WELL AS THE SIZE OF FORT ROZ--THE PRISON WAS BUILT TO INCARCERATE OVER FIVE THOUSAND INMATES AT CAPACITY-- MAKE EITHER SCENARIO JUST AS LIKELY.

AND NON'S ACTIVITIES HAD LONG SINCE BECOME BENEATH NOTICE OF ALL BUT URSA AND ZOD THEMSELVES, ALL THE MORE SO IN THE WAKE OF THEIR RECENT DEFEAT AT SUPERMAN'S HANDS.

FOR CHRISTOPHER, HOWEVER, THIS NEED TO REMAIN HIDDEN IS SECOND TO ONLY ONE THING:

HIS DESIRE TO RETURN TO EARTH AND THE ONLY HAPPINESS, THE ONLY SAFETY, HE HAS EVER KNOWN.

THAT HONOR--IF IT CAN BE CALLED THAT--GOES TO BRAINIAC, AND THE BLACK DAY THAT KANDOR WAS RIPPED FROM KRYPTON.

FOR DECADES PRIOR TO HIS ATTEMPTED CONQUEST OF EARTH, IT WAS BRAINIAC THAT HELD ZOD'S ATTENTION.

WHILE SUPERMAN HAS SUPPLANTED BRAINIAC IN ZOD'S ATTENTIONS...

THOUGH THE ROOM FRIGHTENS CHRISTOPHER, THOUGH THE EQUIPMENT THERE CONFUSES HIM, IT GIVES HIM HOPE.

PERHAPS, IF HE CANNOT LEAVE THE PHANTOM ZONE TO JOIN THOSE HE'S LEFT BEHIND, HE CAN, IN SOME WAY, CONTACT THEM.

CHRISTOPHER DOESN'T KNOW BRAINIAC.

FOR YEARS, HE DEVOTED HIMSELF TO THE STUDY OF HIS ENEMY.

...THE REMNANTS OF HIS PREVIOUS OBSESSION REMAIN, AND THE ROOM IS FILLED WITH THEM.

THOSE BITS AND PIECES OF BRAINIAC TECHNOLOGY THAT HAVE "WASHED UP" WITHIN THE PHANTOM ZONE DURING THE LONG YEARS OF IMPRISONMENT.

EVERYTHING ZOD COULD FIND, ANYTHING THAT MIGHT HELP HIM UNDERSTAND HIS ENEMY, ALL GATHERED HERE.

HE DOESN'T KNOW KANDOR.

BUT WITH ONE DECISION...

...FOR EACH OF THEM.

NOW, IF ANYTHING, THE PAIN IS ALL THE MORE ACUTE.

AS BEFORE, WHEN HE ENTERED THE PHANTOM ZONE, CHRISTOPHER'S BODY GOES HAYWIRE.

NOW IT COMES WITH A SENSE OF LOSS, AS WELL AS SHAME.

ONCE MORE, HE RACES THROUGH YEARS IN A MATTER OF SECONDS.

THARA.

AND FOR THE FIRST TIME, WITH THE MEMORY OF JOY STILL LINGERING...

...CHRISTOPHER FEELS DESPAIR.

THE FEELING IS SHARED BY THARA AK-VAR, NOW WRESTLING WITH KNOWLEDGE THAT EATS AT HER HEART AS MUCH AS HER THOUGHTS.

SO MUCH OF HER LIFE TO THIS POINT HAS BEEN FRAMED BY DOUBT, TO THE POINT THAT, MORE THAN ONCE, SHE HAS QUESTIONED HER OWN SANITY.

IS SHE WHAT THE MONKS AND PRIESTS SAY SHE IS?

IS SHE DESTINED TO BECOME WHAT THEY CLAIM, THE LIVING AVATAR OF THE FLAMEBIRD?

NOW, FOR THE FIRST TIME, SHE IS CERTAIN.

NOW, FOR THE FIRST TIME, SHE TRULY BELIEVES WHAT SHE HAS REFUSED TO ACCEPT.

AND SHE KNOWS WHAT SHE MUST DO.

HOW TO DO IT IS
ANOTHER MATTER
ENTIRELY.

THARA IS NOT SURPRISED WHEN BOTH
ZOR-EL AND ALURA TELL HER THAT WHAT
SHE'S DESCRIBING IS IMPOSSIBLE.

THAT, EVEN IF THER[E]
WAS AN INNOCENT
BOY TRAPPED IN T[HE]
PHANTOM ZONE, A[S]
THARA CLAIMS,
COMMUNICATION WI[TH]
HIM WOULD BE
IMPOSSIBLE.

AS TO ACTUALLY
ENTERING THE ZONE
TO "RESCUE" HIM,
ZOR-EL BELIEVES IN
THE THEORETICAL
POSSIBILITY.

HE HAD EXPLORED [A]
SIMILAR IDEA, THAT [OF]
MANAGED ENTRY A[ND]
EXIT TO THE ZONE, [AS]
A MEANS OF ESCAP[E]
FROM BRAINIAC, US[ING]
ENCOUNTER SUITS A[ND]
A MODIFIED PHANT[OM]
ZONE PROJECTOR[.]

A PROJECT HE HAS SINCE
ABANDONED AT HIS WIFE'[S]
BEHEST AS TOO DANGERO[US]
NOT TO MENTION IMPRACTIC[AL.]

WHILE NEITHER ALURA NOR
ZOR-EL ARE WILLING TO
DISCOUNT THARA'S VISIONS
OUT OF HAND, THEY OFFER
MORE SCIENTIFIC
EXPLANATIONS.

PERHAPS HER IMAGINATION,
INFLUENCED BY THE WORDS
OF THE MONKS AND PRIESTS,
IS RUNNING WILD?

PERHAPS IT WOUL[D]
BE BEST IF SHE
LEFT THE
RELIGIOUS GUILD
AND RETURNED TO
THEIR SERVICE?

TO THEIR
DELIGHT, SHE
AGREES.

AS HEAD OF SECURITY, NO DOOR IS LOCKED.

AS HEAD OF SECURITY, NO ONE QUESTIONS WHERE SHE GOES, OR WHAT SHE DOES.

SHE DOESN'T CONSIDER WHAT SHE'S DOING A BREACH OF TRUST OR AN ABUSE OF POWER.

IT IS SIMPLY AN ISSUE OF DOING WHAT MUST BE DONE.

FOR BOTH OF THEM.

FOR ALL OF THEM.

SINCE HIS CAPTURE, HE HAS BEEN INTERROGATED BY HIS FATHER, TORMENTED BY HIS MOTHER...

...AND TORTURED BY INMATES WHO HAVE USED HIM TO RELIEVE YEARS OF BOREDOM.

FAITH HAS BEEN THE ONLY THING THAT HAS KEPT CHRISTOPHER ALIVE.

HE REMEMBERS THE GIRL, AND THEIR CONNECTION. HE HOLDS ON TO THE WARMTH OF HER THOUGHTS, THE INTIMACY OF HER MIND.

THARA?

THE HOPE THAT SHE WILL COME FOR HIM.

FOR THARA, THE MOMENT IS AN AWFUL CONFLUENCE, LOVE AND HATE COLLIDING IN THE SAME INSTANT.

THE SIGHT OF HER NIGHTWING, BEATEN AND BLOODIED...

YOU!

...AND THE SIGHT OF URSA, THE WOMAN WHO LEFT HER PARENTS TO DIE.

...AK-VAR?

IN LEGEND, FLAMEBIRD AND NIGHTWING ARE DEFINED, TIME AND AGAIN, BY THEIR EMOTIONS.

DEV-EM--

--CUT HER!

JUST AS THEIR PASSION IS LEGENDARY, SO IS THEIR ANGER, AND THEIR SORROW.

BEHIND YOU!

THIS IS ALWAYS AN ELEMENT OF THEIR UNDOING.

IN EACH CYCLE, THEY ARE DESTINED TO END IN TRAGEDY.

gHhn

BUT MOST OFTEN, IN THESE LEGENDS, IT IS THE SAME DOWNFALL.

I'VE GOT YOU--

I KNEW YOU WOULD COME.

TIME AND AGAIN, THE SAME END.

THE PROJECTOR, NON!

ON HER BELT!

LAMEBIRD AND NIGHTWING ARE BETRAYED.

NON...

...PLEASE.

THANK YOU.

NO--

--WHAT ARE YOU DOING?!?

BUT NOT THIS TIME.

NIGHTWING

ALTER EGOS: Lor-Zod, Christopher Kent
BASE OF OPERATIONS: Mobile; formerly the Phantom Zone

POWERS/ABILITIES: A Kryptonian by birth, Nightwing's genetic structure was mutated as a result of his conception and birth in the Phantom Zone. Possessed of the standard Kryptonian power set, he is marginally, if demonstrably, weaker than the rest of his race when under Earth's yellow sun. Kryptonite, while still lethal to him, takes longer to reach full effect. Nightwing has exhibited tactile telekinesis, though if this power is the result of his Phantom Zone birth or his interaction with Brainiac technology, none can say.

HISTORY: Lor-Zod is the only child of **GENERAL ZOD** and **COMMANDER URSA**, born and raised in **FORT ROZ**, in the Phantom Zone. Surrounded by some of Krypton's worst criminals, he would certainly have become one of the most evil creatures the universe had ever seen, but for the machinations of his father. When General Zod used his young son to spearhead an attempted invasion of Earth, the child was discovered by **SUPERMAN**, who immediately forged a strong bond with the boy.

In the care of Superman and Lois Lane, Lor, renamed "Christopher," began a new life, free from the trauma and hardship he had previously experienced. His education by both, along with time spent among Earth's mightiest heroes, had an immediate and profound effect, and instilled in him the passionate desire to follow in Superman's footsteps.

To repel Zod's invasion, Christopher sacrificed his life on Earth, voluntarily returning to the Phantom Zone. Upon reentry, he suffered the first of three bouts of "burst-aging" he has since undergone, his body growing the equivalent of several years in mere seconds. The source of this disorder is unknown, and Nightwing is quite concerned when the next "episode" will occur.

He is currently working with Flamebird, attempting to stop Kryptonian sleeper agents placed on Earth by his father Zod.

FLAMEBIRD

ALTER EGO: Thara Ak-Var
BASE OF OPERATIONS: Mobile; formerly Kandor

Text by GREG RUCKA, art by FERNANDO DAGNINO & RAÚL FERNANDEZ, color by PETE PANTAZIS

POWERS/ABILITIES: Standard Kryptonian power set and vulnerabilities. Additionally, Thara believes herself to be the avatar of the ancient Kryptonian Flamebird, a quasi-religious/mythical beast from the Kryptonian pantheon, best described as a fusion between a phoenix and a dragon, and the eternal mate of the Nightwing, a similar creature composed of shadow and night.

HISTORY: Thara Ak-Var has dreamt of the flames all her life. Born to members of the Military Guild's elite unit Black Zero, Thara was raised on Krypton, with time divided between Kandor and Argo City, the home of her best friend, **KARA ZOR-EL**. The two made an odd pair, Kara a far more scientifically minded girl than her devoutly religious friend. At fourteen, Thara was abducted along with thousands of other Kryptonians when **BRAINIAC** stole the city of Kandor from planet Krypton. The trauma of that event, as well as witnessing the death of her parents (and their subsequent abandonment by their commanding officer, Ursa) in an attempt to rescue her, affected her deeply.

When Brainiac incorporated the captured populace of Argo City into Kandor, Thara was reunited with Kara's parents, **ALURA** and **ZOR-EL**, and became a surrogate daughter to them. It was Zor-El who directed her back to the **RELIGIOUS GUILD** in an attempt to help her recover her faith. Entering the House of Rao, Thara experienced what she maintains was a vision of the Flamebird. Inducted into the Religious Guild and initiated in its mysteries, she shortly after experienced a seizure, and emerged from it convinced that there was a young man trapped in the Phantom Zone — her Nightwing. She effected his rescue, and the two have been together ever since, though Thara has yet to share with him the depth of her feelings, or her religious convictions, for fear of rejection or — worse — that he might believe her insane.